The Ultimate
Leopard
Book for Kids

100+ Amazing Leopard
Facts, Photos & More

Jenny Kellett

BELLANOVA
MELBOURNE · SOFIA · BERLIN

© 2026 Bellanova Books
The Ultimate Leopard Book for Kids
www.bellanovabooks.com

All rights reserved. No part of this book may be reproduced in any form by any electronic or mechanical means including photocopying, recording, or information storage and retrieval without permission in writing from the author.

ISBN: 9786197695014
Imprint: Bellanova Books

Contents

Introduction	4
Leopards - Then and Today	6
Characteristics	14
Their Daily Lives	28
Subspecies of leopard	45
African	46
Indian	50
Javan	52
Arabian	56
Persian	58
Amur	62
Indochinese	64
Sri Lankan	66
Black Panther	70
From Birth to Adulthood	72
Leopards and Humans	86
Leopard Conservation	90
Leopard Quiz	96
Answers	98
Word search	100
Sources	103

INTRODUCTION

The leopard, famous for its beautiful coat, is characterised by its shorter legs and large skull when compared to other wild cats. It is also one of the world's most adaptable cats—able to survive and thrive in a wide range of habitats.

So let's learn more about this amazing feline! Afterwards, test your new knowledge in our leopard quiz.

Are you ready? *Let's go!*

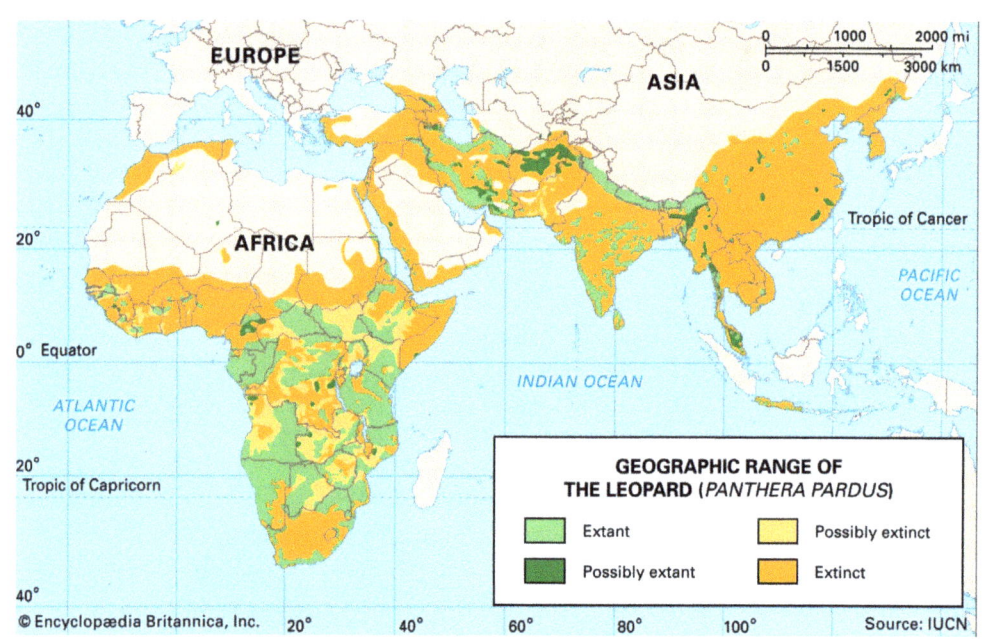

The range of leopards, before and now.

© *Encyclopædia Britannica, Inc.*/*Kenny Chmielewski*

LEOPARDS: THE BASICS

What are leopards and where do they live?

Leopards are very closely related to lions, tigers and jaguars, which are all in the genus *panthera* (all cats in this group can roar). However, despite their name, snow leopards are *not* part of the same group—they are their own species.

...

The closest living relative to the leopard is the lion.

The earliest leopard fossils date back to over 600,000 years ago and were found in Europe. Palaeontologists have also found leopard fossils in Japan.

...

Out of all the big cats, leopards have the largest distribution. You can find leopards living in Africa, Asia and the Caucasus.

...

Leopards in far-eastern Russia live in areas where the winter temperatures can be as low as −25 °C (−13 °F).

An African leopard.

The scientific name for the leopard is *panthera pardus*.

...

Why are they called leopards? The name leopard is believed to have come from the Greek words *leon* (lion) and *pardus* (panther).

...

Although leopards are very adaptable to many environments, they usually prefer rocky areas with dense vegetation where they can hide. Leopards can even be found in some urban areas of sub-Saharan Africa.

Leopards are listed as a **vulnerable species** by the IUCN's *Red List of Threatened Species*. However, several subspecies are critically endangered. Their numbers are shrinking mostly due to habitat destruction and poaching.

...

It might be confusing, but the family of cats called *Leopardus* does not include leopards! It includes cats such as ocelots, margays and Pampas cats.

...

What is the leopard's biggest and only predator? Humans! Sadly, humans hunt leopards for their beautiful fur.

Female leopards are called **leopardesses**.

...

The leopard's geographic range is only 75% of what it was in 1750. Sadly, it is getting smaller and smaller. This is why it's so important to support conservation groups to protect the leopard's future.

...

A group of leopards is called a **leap**.

An African leopardess.

LEOPARD CHARACTERISTICS

Size, features, special traits and more.

By weight, leopards are the strongest of the big cats.

...

Leopards are renowned for their agility. They can reach speeds of up to 58 km/h (36 mph).

...

Leopards are great jumpers! They can spring 6m (19.6 ft) forward through the air.

A charging leopard in South Africa.

© *Rute Martins of Leoa's Photography*

Leopards love lounging around in trees!

As well as jumping, leopards are amazing climbers and they spend a lot of time in trees.

...

Leopards look most similar to jaguars, except they have lighter bodies and their rosettes (spots) are typically smaller and further apart. Their rosettes also don't have spots in the middle of them like jaguars' do.

...

Leopards have soft and thick fur, with even softer fur on their bellies.

Leopards have very good hearing and vision, which makes them great hunters. They can hear 5 times better than humans.

...

The leopard's ears are small and round with black markings on the back. These markings help cubs to see their mothers above tall grass.

...

Leopards are the smallest of the big cats. The average leopard is between 92 to 190 cm (3 to 6.2 ft) in length.

On each foot, leopards have four toes, and the average foot size of a male leopard is 9 cm (3.54 in) and females' are 8 cm (3.14 in).

...

Leopards can see seven times better in the dark than humans.

...

The leopards' rosettes help them to camouflage from predators, particularly when they are hiding in trees.

...

Leopards usually have golden-green or blue eyes with round pupils.

The colour of a leopard's coat depends on where it lives. The **ground colour** of a leopard's fur is more grey-ish in colder climates, and more golden in warmer, tropical climates.

...

A leopard's tail has dark rings around it and a white tip.

...

East African leopards have circular spots, whereas southern African leopards have squareish spots. Asian leopards usually have larger rosettes than African subspecies.

A Sri Lankan leopard cub showing off its tail.

Leopards are great swimmers and will sometimes eat fish and crabs that they catch.

...

On average, leopards weigh 50 to 90 kg (110 to 200 pounds). However, they vary a lot in size and can grow to be much bigger!

...

Male leopards are larger than females, with stockier bodies and larger skulls and paws.

...

The average leopard's tail is around 90 cm (35 in) long, but it's different between each subspecies.

Most leopards have a light ground colour with dark spots and **rosettes**. Rosettes are called this because they look similar to a rose.

...

There are no two leopards that look the same—each has its own individual markings, just like a human fingerprint.

...

Once they reach adulthood, leopards live an average of 12-15 years in the wild, and 22 years in captivity.

The oldest leopard living in captivity is Raven, who was born in Texas on 15 July 1997, making her 25 years old (in 2022).

Leopards, cheetahs and jaguars may look very similar, but it's actually quite easy to tell them apart. Jaguars are the largest, followed by leopards; cheetahs are the smallest. Cheetahs have spots rather than rosettes, and jaguars have larger rosettes with spots in the middle!

LEOPARDS' DAILY LIVES

What do leopards do all day?!

Like all cats, leopards are **carnivores**, meaning they only eat meat.

...

Leopards growl when angry and purr when happy, just like domestic cats.

A leopard enjoying its meal.

Leopards are mostly **solitary** cats; they hunt and live alone, except for females with cubs.

...

In Kruger National Park, South Africa, leopards usually stay around 1 km (0.62 mi) away from other leopards. Male and female leopards will only make contact during mating season.

...

Trees aren't only useful for hiding in—leopards can even hunt from them!
They will blend in with the leaves before pouncing on their prey below.

A leopard marking its territory.

© *Lip Kee*

Leopards live in **home ranges** or **territories**. They mark their territories with scratches on trees, faeces and urine. Although male and female territories sometimes overlap, there will usually be trouble if another leopard of the same gender enters its territory!

...

The size of a leopard's home range depends mostly on how much food it has available. The less food, the larger the home range.

...

Leopards are very elusive and shy, making them hard to find in the wild.

Catching Dinner: The Leopard Way

When a leopard sees a potential meal, it knows what to do!

Leopards are very stealthy and are known as **ambush predators.**

When they spot a meal, they will approach it with its head held low, and then quietly stalk it until it's around five to 10 metres away, and then pounce! If it is larger prey, it will bite its neck or throat to kill it, or if it's something small like a mouse it will just swipe it with its huge paw.

Once they catch up to their prey, they will trip it over and bite its throat until it suffocates or

A leopard with its prey.

crush its skull if it is a smaller animal. They will then drag their prey into a tree— or somewhere else away from other predators—to eat it.

An African leopard showing off its climbing skills.

Asian leopards, which are smaller cats, hunt at different times of the day from tigers to avoid competition for food.

...

Leopards are primarily **nocturnal**, meaning they usually hunt at night. However, they have been seen hunting during the day in parts of western Africa.

...

During their hunting time—between dusk and dawn—leopards can walk up to 75 km (47 mi) in one day, depending on how much food is available.

Despite being nocturnal, leopards still like to occasionally sunbathe during the day!

...

During the day, leopards like to rest. They usually sleep in tree branches, rocky areas, or dense bushes.

...

Leopards prefer to eat medium-sized prey, such as impala, bushbuck and chital (or similar-sized Asian species). However, they occasionally hunt smaller carnivores such as cheetahs and foxes.

Leopards usually drag their prey into trees to stop scavenger animals such as lions and hyenas from stealing them.

...

Leopards can be a problem for farmers as they like to prey on livestock such as sheep and chickens and have been known to attack humans if they get too close.

...

During a documentary called *'Eye of the Leopard'* on National Geographic, a wild leopard was caught killing a baboon. After noticing it had an infant, she carried it into a tree and kept it safe by cuddling and grooming it like she would her own cub.

Leopards are mostly quiet, but they have many different sounds they can use to communicate when needed. These can be harsh coughs, deep purring sounds, meows or throaty growls. A leopard's roar is called 'sawing', as it sounds like sawing wood.

...

Scientists believe that leopards also use visual cues to communicate with each other. For example, the white tips on their tails tell other leopards to 'follow me'.

"Follow me!"

© Lee R. Berger

An African leopard.

Male and female leopards can track each other using scents. The female will release certain pheromones (a special chemical that attracts males) when she is ready to mate.

Leopards don't need to drink water every day to survive. They may only get the chance to drink water every few days, but they can get water from the blood of their prey.

...

Leopards that live in the Kalahari Desert, where there is very little water, sometimes snack on water-rich plants such as succulents and watermelons.

...

Every day, on average, male leopards eat around 3.5 kg (7 lb 11 oz) of food, while females eat around 2.8 kg (6 lb 3 oz) per day.

A Sri Lankan leopard cub.

LEOPARDS: Subspecies

Until 1966, naturalists believed there were up to 27 different subspecies of leopard; however now they agree there are just **nine subspecies**. Leopards have also been crossbred with other big cats to form **hybrids**. The most common is breeding a lioness with a male leopard, producing **leopons**—however, these are not subspecies.

Let's take a quick look to see the differences, and afterwards see you if you can work out the subspecies of the leopards in this book!

AFRICAN LEOPARD

Panthera pardus pardus

The African leopard is the most common subspecies. It lives in most sub-Saharan African countries and a few in North Africa; it has the largest range of all leopard species.

They are nocturnal and are happy living in most habitats except the scorching hot, sandy desert.

Depending on where they live, the coat colour can be very different. They have broken rosettes with a yellow-cream centre over a coat that varies from pale-yellow to dark gold or even black in colour. Their heads, lower limbs and bellies have solid black spots.

The African leopard has the shortest tail of all the subspecies at 68-80 centimetres (27-32 inches) long. It is most similar in size and weight to the Amur leopard.

INDIAN LEOPARD

Panthera pardus fusca

The Indian leopard lives on the Indian subcontinent in Nepal, Bhutan, India and parts of Pakistan. It is one of the five large cats that live in the region. The others are the Asiatic lion, Bengal tiger, snow leopard and the clouded leopard.

If you look at the Indian leopard's coat, you'll notice it has black spots and rosettes on a pale yellow to golden background. The Indian leopard's rosettes are the smallest of the Asian leopard subspecies, fading in colour towards their white underbellies and the insides of their legs.

An Indian leopard. © *Pawan Jaidka*

Compared to African leopards, Indian leopards naturally have a different diet. Their favourite foods are Chital, Sambar and langur—but they are still opportunistic hunters, meaning they aren't picky, so will also prey on Spotted Deer, Nilai, Wild Pig, cattle, hare, dog and porcupine.

JAVAN LEOPARD
Panthera pardus melas

The Javan leopard is an endangered subspecies that can only be found in tropical rainforests on the Indonesian island of Java. Only around 350 are still left in the wild, partly because the population of Java is growing so quickly, and the Javan leopard's habitat is being destroyed.

The Javan leopard is also sometimes called a black panther because it can often have dark fur—however, not all Javan leopards look like this.

Most Javan leopards have a light brown base colour with black spots on their body and silver-grey eyes.

Their diet usually consists of wild boar, barking deer, Java mouse-deer and a few different species of monkeys. Their peak hunting times are between 6-9 am and 3-6 pm.

Sadly, due to Java losing over 90 per cent of its natural habitat, food is becoming scarcer for leopards.

ARABIAN LEOPARD

Panthera pardus nimr

The Arabian leopard is a critically endangered subspecies, meaning it is at a very high risk of extinction. It is the smallest subspecies of leopard and lives in small populations on the Arabian peninsula, in countries such as Yemen and Oman.

The fur of the Arabian leopard varies from pale yellow to deep golden, tawny or grey, with black rosettes. Unlike other subspecies, the Arabian leopard doesn't store its prey in trees. Instead, it takes it into a lair or cave for safe keeping.

An Arabian leopard.
© *Land Rover Our Planet on Flickr.*

They are mostly nocturnal but are sometimes seen during the day. Their usual food is Arabian gazelle, Nubian ibex, Cape hare, rock hyrax, porcupine, Ethiopian hedgehog, and small rodents, birds, and insects.

PERSIAN LEOPARD

Panthera pardus tulliana

The Persian leopard lives in an area known as the Iranian Plateau, which includes Turkey, the Caucasus mountain range, Iran, Turkmenistan and Afghanistan. Also known as the Caucasian or Anatolian leopard, it is an endangered subspecies with less than 1000 living in the wild.

THE ULTIMATE LEOPARD BOOK

Persian leopard cubs.

The Persian leopard's fur is grey and slightly reddish, with large rosettes on its sides and back. The rest of the body has smaller rosettes, while the head and neck has spots. They are slightly different colours depending on where they live, and there are both pale and dark Persian leopards living in Iran.

It is the largest subspecies of leopard and has an average body length of 158 cm (62 in) and a 94 cm (37 in) long tail. They can weigh up to 60 kg (130 lb).

AMUR LEOPARD

Panthera pardus orientalis

The Amur leopard is believed to be the rarest cat species in the world. It lives in southeastern Russia and northern China; less than 110 live in the wild, and about 180 are in captivity.

They are very well adapted to living in cold, snowy climates, and it's easy to tell them apart from other subspecies by their long, thick fur that is perfect for living in the mountains. Their rosettes are large and spread out, particularly

An Amur leopard. © *Art G.*

on their sides, and their winter coats are a darker colour than in summer.

The Amur leopard, also known as the Far Eastern leopard, is quite small, and the males weigh 32.2–48 kg (71–106 lb), while females weigh 25–42.5 kg (55–94 lb).

INDOCHINESE LEOPARD

Panthera pardus delacouri

The Indochinese leopard is native to the mainland of Southeast Asia, in countries such as Thailand, Myanmar and Malaysia, and southern China. It is critically endangered and only lives in 80 per cent of the area it used to just twenty years ago. There are an estimated 973–2,503 living in the wild.

The Indochinese leopard has a beautiful rusty-red ground colour, which is paler at the sides.

An Indochinese leopard at Saigon Zoo, Vietnam.

© *Tomáš Najer*

Their rosettes are quite small and close together, and their fur is short. The further south they live, the darker their fur—with some even appearing almost entirely black.

SRI LANKAN LEOPARD

Panthera pardus kotiya

The Sri Lankan leopard lives on the island of Sri Lanka in various habitats, including tea plantations, forests, people's home gardens and eucalyptus plantations. They are widespread and are listed as vulnerable, meaning that their numbers are declining, but they are not yet at risk of extinction.

It has a pale, tawny or rusty-coloured coat, with rosettes smaller than the Indian leopard's.

A Sri Lankan leopard. © *Dinuka Kavinda*

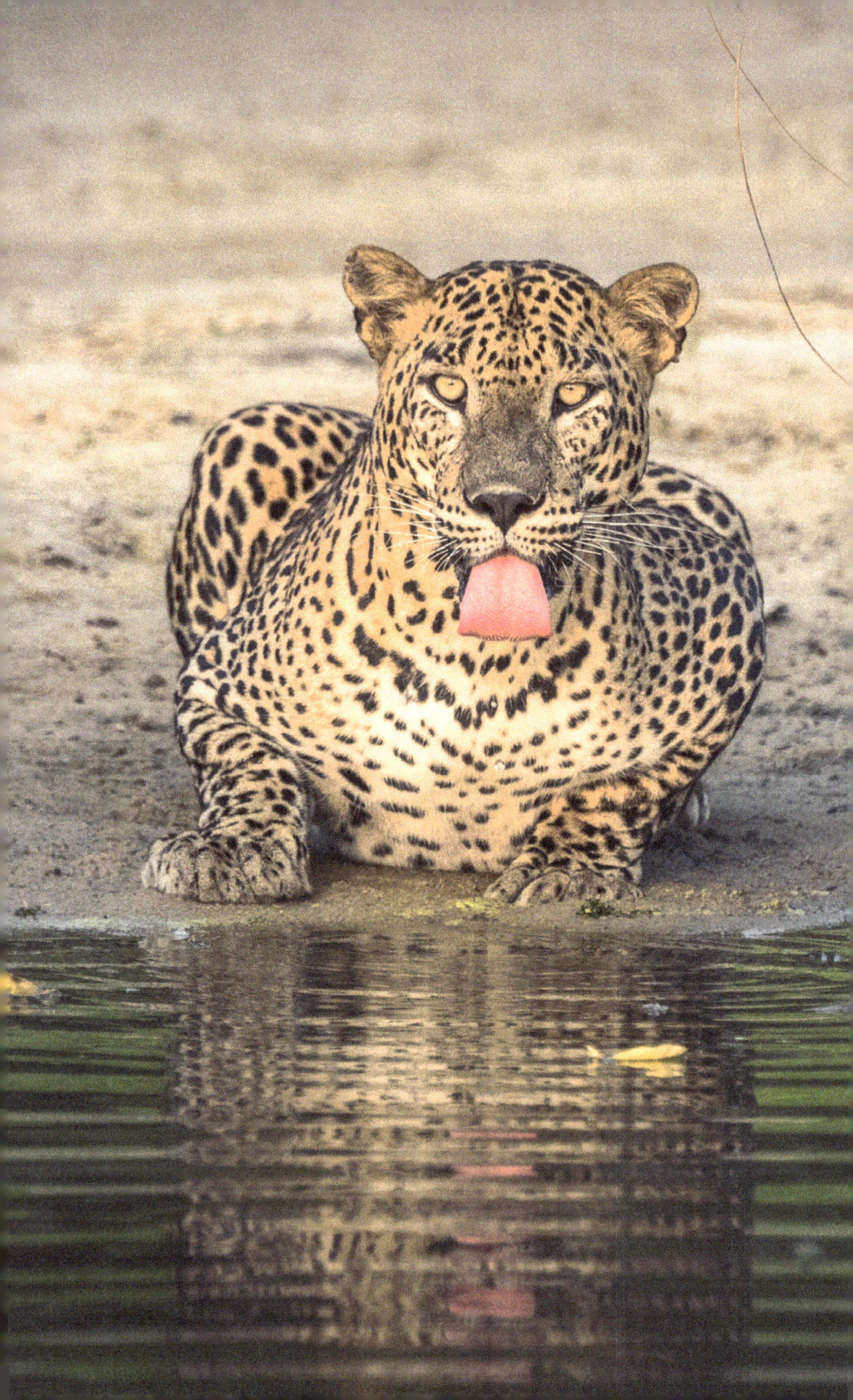

The Sri Lankan leopard is quite large, which scientists believe is because they are apex predators, meaning they don't have any natural predators, so they have never had much competition for food. Sri Lankan leopardesses weigh an average of 56 kg (64 lb.), while the males are around 56 kg (124 lb.), although they can be much larger.

Like other subspecies, the Sri Lankan leopard isn't too fussy about what it eats. Still, its usual diet consists of Sri Lankan axis deer (when living in dry areas), sambar, barking deer, wild boar and monkeys.

BLACK PANTHER

The black panther is not a subspecies of leopard as such. Any leopard that is **melanistic**, meaning it has a gene that causes extra black pigment in its skin or fur, is known as a black panther. Black panthers can also be melanistic jaguars!

Black leopards still have rosettes. However, it's hard to see them as their ground colour is also black. They are most common in Asia's tropical rainforest, and any subspecies of leopard can be a 'black panther', however, it's more common in

A female black leopard. © *Gary Whyte*

the Indian and Indochinese leopards. In Africa, black panthers are the continent's rarest big cat. Black jaguars live in the Americas in Mexico, Paraguay, Costa Rica and Paraguay.

FROM BIRTH TO ADULTHOOD

Baby leopards are some of the most adorable in the animal kingdom, so let's learn more about their early lives.

Baby leopards are called cubs.

...

When a cub is born, it is almost hairless and weighs just 500 to 600 grams (17 to 21 ounces).

A leopardess with her cub.

An African leopard cub. © *Chris Eason*

The **gestation period** (how long the pregnancy lasts) of a leopardess is around three months or 96 days.

...

Leopardesses usually give birth to a litter of two or three cubs. They give birth in a safe place such as a cave, hollow tree trunk or rock crevice.

...

During the first eight weeks of their lives, cubs are hidden away by their mothers in a **den** or **lair** to keep them safe from predators. Dens can be anything from a natural cave to an abandoned aardvark hole.

Mothers keep moving their cubs between safe spots until they are ready to go out on their own.

...

Leopard cubs don't leave their mother's den until they are three months old.

...

Cubs suckle their mother's milk for around three months. After six or seven weeks, they'll have their first taste of meat.

...

At 12-18 months old, leopard cubs are ready to live independently. However, they usually stay with their mothers until they are two years old.

An Amur leopard cub.
© Tambako The Jaguar @ Flickr

A leopard cub showing us its teeth.

Although leopards can breed throughout the year, they usually give birth during the rainy season when there is more food.

...

Leopard cubs are greyish in colour and their spots are barely visible.

...

Cubs use an **'urr-urr'** sound to communicate with their mothers.

It's a tough life in the wild. Sadly, around 41-50 per cent of wild leopard cubs die before they're one year old.

...

Leopard cubs are born blind. They open their eyes when they are around four to nine days old, and their eyes are bright blue for the first few months.

...

Cubs' fur usually looks quite dark as their spots are much closer together; they appear lighter as they grow bigger and their spots spread out. Their fur is usually longer and softer than adults, too.

A black leopard cub.

During the first few months of her cubs' lives, the leopardess only hunts very close to her den.

...

Around three months old, cubs start following their mothers on hunts.

LEOPARDS AND HUMANS

For thousands of years, humans and leopards have had a special relationship. They are depicted in artwork, folklore and mythology in many countries around the world.

The Persian leopard is the national animal of Iran (jointly with the Asiatic Lion).

...

The leopard is featured on the coat of arms of many different countries, including Benin, Malawi, Somalia and the Democratic Republic of Congo.

Leopards don't hunt humans, and they are less likely to attack humans than lions and tigers are. However, they will attack humans if they feel threatened or if there is a food shortage.

...

In the book *The Jungle Book* by Rudyard Kipling, there is an Indian black panther called 'Bagheera'. There are also two Disney movies based on the book—from 1967 and 2016.

...

In another Rudyard Kipling book, *How the Leopard Got His Spots*, a leopard living in South Africa was born with no spots. You have to read the story to find out what happens next!

THE ULTIMATE LEOPARD BOOK

Early Byzantine mosaic of a leopard.
© *Guillaume Piolle*

Although leopards aren't the most dangerous cats, there have been some famous man-eating leopards in the past. The best known was the **Leopard of Panar**, who was responsible for at least 400 deaths in the early 20th century!

...

The Ancient Romans would keep leopards in captivity and use them in executions of criminals.

...

Leopards have been tamed and trained to perform in circuses. Luckily, in most Western countries this is now illegal.

In the 13th century, several leopards were kept at the Tower of London **menagerie** (an early zoo) by King John of England.

...

In Greek mythology the leopard was often associated with the god **Dionysus** who used a leopard for transportation.

...

In the Benin Empire (a former kingdom of southwestern Nigeria), the leopard was considered to be the 'king of the world'.

...

At the 2014 Sochi Winter Olympics, a leopard (alongside a hare and a polar bear) was the mascot for the games.

A mosaic showing Greek God Dionysus riding on a leopard. 4th Century BC, Greece.

LEOPARD CONSERVATION

Sadly, leopards have a difficult and uncertain future. Despite leopards being the most common big cats in the world, they are still at risk of extinction. In just the last 22 years, their range has decreased by 31 per cent.

Some subspecies, including the Amur leopard, are critically endangered and without the help of conservation groups, will not continue to exist within our lifetimes. The main risks facing leopards are the destruction of their habitats and poaching (illegal killing by humans).

Some of the organisations working on leopard conservation.

Fortunately, there are many people and organisations who care a lot about the future of leopards. And everyone, including you, has an opportunity to help.

How can you help leopards?

Leopards need help from people just like you to raise awareness of their problems.

You can support many organisations, including *Panthera.org, WWF, African Wildlife Foundation*, and the *Wild Cats Conservation Alliance*.

Through these organisations, you have opportunities to adopt a leopard, donate money and learn more about other ways you can help.

International Leopard Day is celebrated on **May 3rd** each year.

It's purpose is to raise global awareness of the problems that leopards face. But, that's not the only day we should be thinking about leopards!

Here are some ways you can help protect them:

- Instead of gifts on your birthday, ask for donations to your favourite leopard charity!
- Hold a bake sale to raise money.
- Be a leopard ambassador! Share information about the problems leopards face on your social media and speak to friends and family to spread the word.
- Adopt a leopard (virtually, of course!) through the organizations mentioned before.
- Check with your local zoo to see what projects they're involved in and how you can help.

LEOPARD quiz

Now test your knowledge in our leopard quiz! Answers are on page 98.

1 What is a female leopard called?

2 Which is smaller, a cheetah or a leopard?

3 Leopards can roar. True or false?

4 What is the leopards closest living relative?

5 What is the scientific name for the leopard?

6 What is a group of leopards called?

7 How fast can leopards run?

8 What colour are leopards eyes?

9 How long do leopards live for?

10 How many subspecies of leopard are there? Bonus points if you can name them!

11 Which is the largest subspecies of leopard?

12 Which subspecies is most critically endangered?

13 Which subspecies of leopard lives in Indonesia?

14 How long is the leopardesses gestation period?

An Indian leopard.

15 How many cubs do leopardesses usually have?

16 When do leopard cubs first leave their mother's den?

17 When do leopard cubs open their eyes?

18 Which subspecies of leopard is the national animal of Iran?

19 What is the difference between leopard and jaguar rosettes?

20 Which leopard subspecies has the shortest tail?

ANSWERS

1. Leopardess.
2. Cheetah.
3. True.
4. Lion.
5. panthera pardus
6. A leap.
7. Up to 58 km/h (36 mph).
8. Blue or a golden-green.
9. 12-15 years in the wild, and 22 years in captivity.
10. Nine. African, Indian, Sri Lankan, Javan, Arabian, Persian, Amur and Indochinese.
11. Persian.
12. The Amur leopard.
13. The Javan leopard.
14. 96 days, or three months.
15. Two to three.
16. When they are three months old.
17. Between four and nine days old.
18. Persian leopard.
19. Jaguar rosettes are larger with black spots in the middle.
20. The African leopard.

A Sri Lankan leopard.

Leopard
WORD SEARCH

W	V	G	F	D	S	A	H	J	U	T	R
F	U	D	R	H	F	Q	P	Y	H	F	V
D	L	P	A	N	T	H	E	R	A	D	D
S	N	C	F	F	P	K	J	O	P	C	W
Y	E	G	F	E	Q	A	F	S	J	U	N
T	R	H	D	F	L	Q	N	E	T	B	V
R	A	E	W	A	A	I	C	T	D	S	X
W	B	S	F	E	M	Z	N	T	H	K	W
Q	L	D	G	W	U	Z	X	E	J	E	R
L	E	O	P	A	R	D	E	S	S	Y	R
A	S	D	Q	E	P	Y	J	F	S	T	T
D	C	A	R	N	I	V	O	R	E	D	E

Can you find all the words below in the word search puzzle on the left?

LEOPARDESS	FELINES	VULNERABLE
ROSETTES	PANTHERA	CUBS
PANTHER	AMUR	CARNIVORE

THE ULTIMATE LEOPARD BOOK

WORD SEARCH SOLUTION

	V								
	U								
	L	P	A	N	T	H	E	R	A
	N		F		P		O		C
	E			E		A		S		U
	R				L		N	E		B
	A				A	I		T		S
	B				M		N	T	H	
	L				U			E		E
L	E	O	P	A	R	D	E	S	S		R
	C	A	R	N	I	V	O	R	E	

SOURCES

Kellett, Jenny. ***The Big Big Cats Book for Kids*** (2020). Available from Amazon.

OneKind, D. et al. (2022) ***Amazing Facts about Leopards | OneKindPlanet Animal Education & Facts, OneKindPlanet.*** Available at: https://onekindplanet.org/animal/leopard/ (Accessed: 7 June 2022).

Leopard | National Geographic (2022). Available at: https://www.nationalgeographic.com/animals/mammals/facts/leopard (Accessed: 7 June 2022).

leopard | Description, Habitat, & Facts (2022). Available at: https://www.britannica.com/animal/leopard (Accessed: 7 June 2022).

What is the difference between the African Leopard, the North Chinese Leopard, the Persian Leopard and the Snow Leopard? (2018). Available at: https://similarbutdifferentanimals.com/2018/11/17/what-is-the-difference-between-the-african-leopard-the-north-chinese-leopard-the-persian-leopard-and-the-snow-leopard (Accessed: 7 June 2022).

African leopard - Wikipedia (2022). Available at: https://en.wikipedia.org/wiki/African_leopard (Accessed: 7 June 2022).

FACTS ABOUT JAVAN LEOPARD (2022). Available at: https://www.balisafarimarinepark.com/facts-about-javan-leopard/ (Accessed: 9 June 2022).

Meet Our Animals | Amur leopard (2022). Available at: https://philadelphiazoo.org/animals/amur-leopard/#:~:text=The%20World's%20Rarest%20Big%20Cat,and%20only%20180%20in%20captivity. (Accessed: 13 June 2022).

Black panther - Wikipedia (2022). Available at: https://en.wikipedia.org/wiki/Black_panther (Accessed: 13 June 2022).

10 leopard facts! - National Geographic Kids (2019). Available at: https://www.natgeokids.com/uk/discover/animals/general-animals/leopard-facts/ (Accessed: 13 June 2022).

(2022) Escapesafarico.com. Available at: https://www.escapesafarico.com/post/international-leopard-day-2021-celebrating-leopards (Accessed: 13 June 2022).

Facts About Leopards (2014). Available at: https://www.livescience.com/27403-leopards.html (Accessed: 14 June 2022).

THE ULTIMATE LEOPARD BOOK

We hope you learned some awesome facts about leopards!

Which was your favourite?

Visit us at www.bellanovabooks.com for more great books, resources and regular giveaways!

ALSO BY JENNY KELLETT

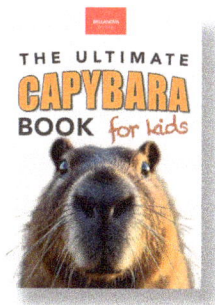  

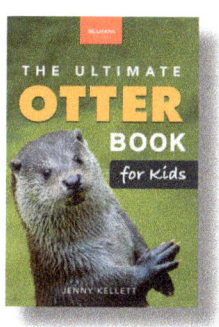  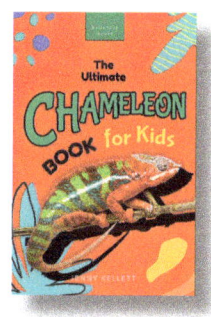

... and more!

Available at

www.bellanovabooks.com

and all major online bookstores.

www.ingramcontent.com/pod-product-compliance
Lightning Source LLC
LaVergne TN
LVHW050131080526
838202LV00061B/6470